LYME REGIS CAMERA

JOHN FOWLES

LYME REGIS CAMERA

LITTLE, BROWN AND COMPANY
Boston · Toronto · London

1. Broad Street in the 1880s

First American Edition

First published in 1990 by the Dovecote Press Ltd.

Library of Congress Catalog Card Number 91-5251

Library of Congress Cataloging-in-Publication information is available.

10 9 8 7 6 5 4 3 2 1

Published simultaneously in Canada by Little, Brown & Company (Canada) Limited

Printed in Singapore

Frontispiece
Lyme under cloud, photographed by Paul Penrose in 1981.

Contents

Introduction

It sometimes seems, at least in this century, that everyone who came to Lyme attempted to photograph it, though seldom with much artistic success. This was hardly the would-be Cartier-Bressons' fault. Lyme, with its wild coasts, so open southwards to the sea, may seem very charming in the mind, but in harsh reality it is heavily loaded against the camera. Outside the Cobb it is painfully short of imposing monuments. It almost completely lacks picturesque houses. The rapid turn-over of its population since at least 1800 (constant emigration of natives, equally constant inflow of outside 'settlers', now mainly the retired) is the despair of any local historian orientated towards the past. So also for his architectural equivalent are the endless changes of fronts and facades in our older streets. Walk through many Broad Street and Coombe Street shops and houses, from the front to the back or upstairs, and you pass through several centuries. Lyme has always had to obey a rule of the oldest profession. If you want fresh customers, put on fresh faces. Those transient faces partly explain the acute brevity of much local memory. I am grateful to Jack Wiscombe and Cecil Quick for helping to remedy that.

The pursuit of today, however cheap and foolish, at the cost of yesterday, however venerable and beautiful, is perhaps normal with seaside resorts like Lyme, so totally dependent on its one modern 'industry': tourism. We lack the old houses and long-rooted families, the stability and sense of tradition, of most inland towns. Even that last word is ambiguous. Lyme *is* a town historically; but in almost everything else, as many casual visitors in the busy season do not realize, it is a village. Its winter population is only some 3,500.

Old photographs gain a special value. Lyme is lucky in possessing some of the first in Dorset, from the 1850s. Others here, such as that due to a Mr Allnut coming to Lyme on his honeymoon in 1911 (and so providing that invaluable thing, an exact dating) we owe to chance – and the kindness of an elderly daughter, who sent us the set. The Museum has its own large collection, and possesses the *Lister Thesaurus*, a priceless compilation of earlier this century made by Gulie Lister and Blanche Palmer ... a great mass of notes, postcards, drawings and photographs of an earlier Lyme.

Among the earliest professional photographers here were the Misses Angelina and Emily Barrett of the Butter Market, who appear as 'photographic artists' in the Kelly's Directory of 1865. A naive little photo of the child Sophie Hoare on their stamped card must date from at least twenty years earlier. F. Boswell, who advertised himself as occupying 'the door above the church' (57 Church Street) in 1869 was also early. He seems to have disappeared about 1875. His establishment was taken over by F. W. Shephard, perhaps best known for the pictures in Mate's *Illustrated Lyme Regis* of 1902, where he advertised. H. and J. Walter of the grandly named Photographic Institute, Broad Street, were also functioning from the 1860s.

Other photos here, especially those from the marvellous Frith series, come from two important sources in Dorchester: the parish collections in respectively the County Museum and the Central Reference Library, whose assistance I gratefully acknowledge (as also that of Jo Draper) in selecting the pictures in this book. Nevertheless, it cannot be exhaustive, indeed the very opposite. We have had to reject countless other photographs, and largely exclude all from our two 'sister' villages, Charmouth in Dorset and Uplyme in Devon.

Some of the shots here may by modern standards

verge on the banal; yet these views of people, streets and houses that no longer exist or are profoundly altered seem, at least to me, to be inherently magical. Yes, change is natural, life is fundamentally fluid; water, not the solid flesh and bones we should like to think. But there is something eternally time-defying, not fluid at all, at the heart of photographs; of a lost dimension, not ours. How quickly and immensely things change! Yet *this* can surely never change! It was so; and somewhere it must remain always

so, the vanished past miraculously switched back on, the gone made present again, yesterday mysteriously become now. Books of past photographs are a little what graveyards were for the Victorians: where we think of what we are, and meditate on that meditation-spurning thing, the eternal leaping torrent of life.

JOHN FOWLES
Lyme Regis

Acknowledgements

I am grateful to the Trustees of Lyme Regis Museum for allowing me to make use of the Museum photographic Collection. All of the photographs come from the Museum, with the following exceptions: Maurice Bishop: 131; Sue and Stuart Case: 34, 88; Ken Gollop: 89; the Dorset County Library: 53, 81; the Curator and Trustees of the Dorset Natural History and Archaeological Society, Dorset County Museum, Dorchester: 51, 52, 55, 65, 66, 70, 84, 87, 106, 107; Brenda Lang: 36; Roger Mayne: 95, 97, 117; John Oldfield: 132; Paul Penrose: Frontispiece, 73.

Early Photographs

These photographs are among the very first in Dorset. Some may be dated to at least the early 1850s. The originals, on glass, are impossible to attribute and have largely vanished; fortunately they were copied in later Victorian times. The *Lister Thesaurus* suggests that several were by James Moly (see 14), but we lack conclusive evidence.

2. One of the most aged photographs of Broad Street. The Lion is not yet Royal and the gleam of the 'shute lake' (see next picture) may be seen on the right.

3. The young man stands beside the 'shute lake', the stream in a gutter that before pipes brought running water down Broad Street. It had been constructed in 1551, and was destroyed soon after 1850. Many of the lower buildings on the left, which held the then post office, were destroyed in the 1889 fire.

4. The Lion was visited by Edward, Prince of Wales, on 25 September 1856. It did not grant itself the 'Royal' at once, but first put the prince's plumes over the sign, just to be seen here. Broad Street is unmade. Girls went to the Turles' school, whose door and steps stand just beyond the Lion.

5. The Square, showing the Pilot Boat and the quaint old Fossil Depot, lost in 1913, with its whalebone. The tall building is the wine importers Goddard's (later Southwood's), which preceded the Rock Point Inn.

6. Cobb Bay in the early 1850s. The Lower Walk or Cart-road is not yet built. The projecting part is of the old West Fort, built in 1627. It had disappeared by 1863.

7. The same view. A painting exists of the running ashore in a storm of the *Mary Ann* in January 1851, which dates this and the next photograph of it and other wreckage. The *Mary Ann*, a smack lengthened into a schooner, was built by Henry Chard, the Lyme shipbuilder, in 1809.

8. The *Mary Ann*, 1851. The little figures are engaged in an old activity of poverty-ridden Lyme after storms: coal-picking. Much coal was then imported from the north-east. The sight of ships in full sail in a waterless harbour, as here, was also common: after gales canvas needed drying out.

9. *(Above)* Cobb Bay and the Walk (now Marine Parade) from the Cobb. Library Cottage was for long the last house on the Walk. In its first form it was a circulating library. The taller house next to it is Argyle House, an earlier sea baths. The photograph lacks the truckway of 1853 at this point, so is probably earlier.

10. *(Opposite top)* Shipping in the Cobb at about the same date. It remained a busy minor port all through the century.

11. *(Opposite bottom)* This revealing early picture of the slope behind the Cobb shows the truckway that once ran out from the Cement Works to the landing quay. It seems to have been constructed about 1853. The photograph also shows the long white wall of old Stile Lane running down to the Cobb hamlet. The house just beyond it is the ill-fated Cliff House, demolished in the slip of 1962. Higher still, to the left, is walled Belmont. Its present garden was then a horse paddock.

12. *(Above)* Another very old picture of the Cobb. Ozone Terrace is not yet built. The cluster of little boats moored close to the ship at left against the North Wall are stoneboats: sea-quarrying was an important activity in Lyme up to 1914. It had nothing to do with the Cement Works.

13. *(Left)* Near the junction of the main road to Uplyme and the northern end of Haye Lane. The houses to left and right, now much altered, are Lydwell House and Solways. The walk to here from Lyme used to be known as the Ladies' Mile, because of its comparative flatness.

People

14. *(Above)* James Moly of Langmoor, 1826-1910. The photograph is by his friend Pulman. Born in Hawkchurch, Moly was said to be the handsomest man in Dorset. He went to Roberts' school in Lyme. Keen on wildfowling and fishing, and an ardent pteridophile (lover of ferns), he gave £400 to Lyme at Blanche Palmer's suggestion, which bought the gardens still named after his house, the old manor of Charmouth. It is not truly known whether he, or some other friend like Pulman, took some of the photos in the previous section.

15. *(Following page)* Sam Govier 1855-1943 (shoeing the horse) in his forge on the present site of Woolworths. Govier was immortalised by Whistler in his painting *The Master Smith of Lyme*. He gave up his forge about 1928. There are several other Whistler paintings and etchings of it.

17. *(Above)* The Rev. Frederick Parry Hodges, Vicar of Lyme between 1830 and 1880, when he died. Known as the Doctor, less kindly (for his autocratic manner) as the 'Bishop of Lyme', Hodges was of the Fane family, who 'ran' Lyme corruptly for most of the 18th and the start of the 19th century; yet was firmly evangelical and Low Church despite his upper-class upbringing and origins.

16. *(Above)* Robert Jones, 1785-1870, with his housekeeper. He remembered the execution of the French king and queen in 1793, and semaphored the news of Waterloo from the Look-out at Charton. His grandparents ran the old Lion in Lyme. He and his brother lived in a now lost house in Silver Street, where they made their own cider in the 'ring-'us' (wring-house).

18, 19. *(Below)* This old couple, James and Mary Hallett, are perhaps most famous for their daughter Selina, who won the 1920 prize essay on old Lyme. James, a shoemaker, was also coachman to Captain Benett of St Andrew's. They first lived in Silver Street, and later in Pound Road.

20. *(Above)* The Lyme Volunteers, winners of the Brigade Challenge Cup at Portland in 1896. This was the year before Fred Britton took over as Company Sergeant Major. The 'clock' was a range and wind indicator. There are many well-known faces among the Volunteers. The two sitting extreme left are blacksmith Sam Govier and Jack Holmes, who had been perhaps the last Lyme schooner-boy in the 1870s. The man with the white beard behind is Mark Lawton, who once ran the Mill Green silk factory and was landlord of the Angel.

21. *(Left)* CSM Fred Britton of the Royal Garrison Artillery, who drilled the Lyme Volunteers before the First World War. He is in the Drill Hall with the gun used for 'repository' – practise in mounting and dismounting. There were a hundred Volunteers at Lyme. Britton was later landlord of the Ship Inn in Coombe Street. His wife taught music, and played at Assembly Rooms dances.

22. *(Above)* The Lyme Fire Brigade in 1908, taken before the conservatory of the Alexandra hotel. The captain of the brigade was Foxwell, seated second from left. First on the left is Jack Holmes, while on his right stands Bob Rattenbury, who had been the sole survivor of the *Olive Branch* wreck of 1893. Her loss (off Lincolnshire) hit the town hard. Sam Govier is seated extreme right.

23. *(Right)* Caroline Philpot, who gave the Museum to the town in 1921. She had inherited it from her uncle, T. E. D. Philpot, who died in 1918. Mayor in 1890-1, and himself great- nephew of the three fossil-collecting Miss Philpots of earlier in the century, he was not locally esteemed; yet that Lyme needed a museum seems to have been his idea.

24. The walking funeral. An old Lyme custom, because of the hills. This one was of John Groves, landlord of the Royal Lion, in 1904.
Vicar Hodges killed this practice, by announcing he would leave all walking funerals to his curates. He conducted only 'proper' carriage
ones. Rendall's grocery may be seen to the right.

25. The little girl centrally to the front was Rosa Rendall. Born about 1887, a red-haired child with a mischievous temper, she also was immortalised by Whistler as *The Little Rose of Lyme*. They say she ran away when Whistler first approached her in Broad Street in 1895 saying he wished to paint her. She thought he meant, to cover her in paint.

26. Rosie Rendall in 1911. News of the Ballet Russe and its fashions had evidently reached Exeter, where she by then worked as a milliner, and later married.

27. Sally 'Granny' Cox, *née* French, shown here in 1911 outside her cottage on East Cliff, was born in 1817. She died aged 97. She had worked, aged only eight, at the Silk Factory in Mill Green for sixpence a week, winding bobbins. Later she stoked the furnace of the East Cliff Gasworks. The jasmine-bush outside her cottage, seen in the background here, was famous.

28. In 1913 there was a lock-out at the Cement Works on Monmouth Beach, and an indignant march of protest. The banner reads: '375 men, women and children depend (on) the works' success. Give us work. Why take our bread away'. The widening of Bridge Street this year may be seen behind. Alas, the works did close down for ever in 1914.

29. On the right Wyatt Wingrave, who founded the Museum at Lyme, lectures on ammonites. A once distinguished ear, throat and nose specialist from Coventry, he became almost completely deaf. His main interest when he retired to Lyme in 1913 lay in ammonites. It was his enthusiasm that very largely got the Museum started. He lived near the beach at the Cobb, at what is now the Harbour Inn.

30. Walter Abbott, the Town Crier, famous for his penetrating voice. The 'deaf' gentleman is E. J. Leeming, who owned the Stile House Hotel. A Lyme friend had been in the Luton straw boater trade, whence his hat.

31. Mrs Bowdidge or Burridge, landlady of the Dolphin, a once well-known but now lapsed Mill Green beerhouse, with her son-in-law and daughter, Mr and Mrs Ted James. She and Mrs Lawton, the landlady of the neighbouring pub, the Angel, were both notably strict and yet charitable towards their poorer neighbours and customers. They were the two 'saints' of Mill Green.

32. The Dolphin's reputation among the more respectable was not too good, as it became the tramps' house in Lyme. Chafey or Hitchcock, known throughout Lyme as 'The Bird', though not a 'roadie', was one of its characters. He used to go along the cliffs and capture a young jackdaw, then tame it and carry it on his shoulder.

33. William Curtis. Stories about the eccentric Curtis family are legion. They worked above all as fishermen from Back Beach; some sold fossils. Two brothers were once left half shares in a boat. One of them promptly went down to the Back Beach and sawed it in half. Like many Lyme characters, they all had nicknames.

34. Sarah Benett (1850-1924) was a granddaughter of Captain Benett of St Andrew's, a distinguished Navy man. His family were important in old Lyme society. Sarah was strongly committed politically and became a leading suffragette in the pre-1914 days. Her crippled brother Newton was one of the better artists of late Victorian Lyme

35. Blanche Palmer, 1852-1920. The photo is of about 1896. Her father, Anthony, lived like her at No 12 Silver Street, and kept an antiquarian shop. He was one of a group of like-minded men in the area: Moly, Pulman, the Axminster artist Newbery. Blanche remained a staunch Christian and greatly helped another erudite spinster, Gulie Lister, in compiling the *Thesaurus*.

36. The man on the left is W. D. Lang of Charmouth, the most eminent local geologist of this century. He is talking with Gulie Lister. The pair on the right are the Hardings, father and daughter. The latter, Gwen, was the first person to see *HMS Formidable*'s forlorn lifeboat on New Year's Day, 1915.

37. *(Left)* Dr Collins, a scientist who lived at St Andrew's after the Benetts left. This photograph was taken on his 80th birthday in 1912.

38. *(Below)* The Lyme Infants class of 1926. Several well-known Lyme names are in this little group: Gollop, Emmett, Hodder, Hitchcock, Loveridge, Broom. The taller boy standing against the wall fifth from the left is Cecil Simmonds, later to be a respected Coombe Street butcher. The little girl next to him is Ruby Quick, Cecil Quick's wife.

The Town

The town looks back to the east, as if still not quite sure in which county, Dorset or Devon (whose boundary is only a few steps away), it belongs. The doubt lingers through all its history. Yet some old landmarks, both natural and manmade, remain.

39. A photograph of about 1895 shows some of the landmarks. The square building against the sea to the left is the old grammar school, built in 1834, now flats. Below it is the Church Street National School, opened in 1892. At the extreme right is the triangular pediment, echoing distant Golden cap, of the Methodist chapel, demolished in 1978. The old dissenters' chapel with its two eye-windows and long roof, since 1755 a bulwark of Lyme's longlasting opposition to the Church of England, lies in hidden Coombe Street to the left. Coombe Street was the heart of old Lyme, when the town was at its mercantile height.

40. A Frith of 1892 looking down on the Cobb and its hamlet. Ozone Terrace is not yet complete. The conical Monmouth beach brickworks kiln may be seen, and the long roofs of the two lifeboat houses. The foundations of the cottage in the foreground were visible until twenty years ago, but are now smothered. The Ware Cliffs path runs right beside them, under Holmbush Knap. Devon is only a field away.

41. The old Charmouth Road. It is heading towards the Devil's Bellows, the cutting down into Charmouth. The road was closed to traffic in 1924, but was open to pedestrians until 1937. This used to be the normal way into Lyme.

42. Another view from the other direction of the old road into Lyme. The fragility of the foxmould soil here can be seen.

43. This is Colway Manor, before the fire of 1921, on whose ruins the present house was rebuilt.

44. Frost's Corner, the old Turnpike Cottage at the top of Colway Lane, photographed in 1911. The modern Charmouth road, opened in 1928, goes to the right as seen in this photograph. The photographer stands in the old road, which led straight across Black Ven.

45. Fairfield Cottage on the Charmouth Road, in 1911, opposite Fairfield. Its coachman and gardener lived here.

46. *(Left)* Summerhill, only recently demolished, in mid-Victorian times. Built by an early Lyme speculator about 1819 in imitation of Georgian Weymouth, in 1924 it became A. S. Neill's celebrated school. He retained the Lyme name when the school moved elsewhere.

47. *(Below)* Little Park, from due west. Summerhill lies across the valley opposite, and the white wall of the cemetery may be seen left of that. This picturesque old house was the home of Francis Palgrave, the famous anthologist.

48. The Gables in Church Street. It was the Cottage Hospital from 1897 on, and was assisted by the Lister family. It now lets holiday flats. Just beyond is the entrance to the 1892 School.

49. A 1904 view of Monmouth Square, popularly known as Cats' Park. It was given to the town in 1907; the closer houses have gone. The building at the end of the street to the right was the Duke of Monmouth Refreshment Rooms, a temperance café. Old Lyme had absurdly too many pubs.

50. This old photograph shows Caddy's team of men near the completion of the building of the Museum, at about the turn of the century.

51. A photograph of about 1914 showing Mill Green, the poorer quarter of Lyme, and the hill west. The larger building right, now Jordan Flats, was a cloth factory, and later a laundry. A first house, built in 1913, may be seen beyond at the junction of the as yet undeveloped Hill and View Roads.

52. A turn of the century view from the Guildhall down to the opening of Coombe Street. The shop at the end has disappeared.

53. The southern end of Coombe Street. The houses to the left all disappeared in the 1920s. The one behind shows slate-cladding, the method devised to counter the crumbling of Blue Lias stone. Brown's Grocery, now Brian Langdon's Fossil Shop, is to the right. Lyme's famous old annual celebration in aid of the Cobb, the Cobb Ale, took place in just this area.

54. Bridge Street during the laying of the electricity cables in 1909. This ancient street, less than eight feet across at its narrowest, was an early victim of the new car.

55. Bridge Street in 1913. The demolition of its seaward side for widening revealed a medieval chapel once serving the bridge over the Buddle. Its aumbry arch may be seen in the wall centrally. It is now in the Museum, to be seen just behind.

57. *(Above)* A Frith of 1892. The boys and girl with arm akimbo are standing just before Gosling Bridge between the King's Mill Leat, a very early feature of Lyme, and the Lim. The old Angel Inn may be seen beyond. Mill Green leads up the hill beyond, while the wall left is the beginning of Sherborne Lane.

56. *(Opposite)* The Fossil Depot, with its whalebone. Contrary to general belief it had nothing to do with Mary Anning, and did not exist until after her death in 1847. It was demolished in 1913. For many years in the hands of the Dollins, it ended in those of Sidney Curtis, who sold both fresh and fossil fish side by side. His wife, 'Long Titch', standing here in the doorway, was well known for her dancing.

58. This strange little tower just east of Gosling Bridge is a relic of Lyme's long defunct cloth trade. It was used for fulling and drying. The twin gables beyond are of the Congregational Chapel in Coombe Street, now Dinosaurland.

59. Lyme Guest House, at the foot of Hill Road. It is here the Earl of Westmorland is said to have stayed on his very occasional visits to Lyme – usually to supervise the (fixed) elections in the town he 'owned'. It was Miss Lord's dame school in Victorian times.

60. Woodmead Road to be, looking north-east and leading down to the Lim and Windsor Terrace, perhaps about 1905. On Philpot land and laid out by Alben Wiscombe, it was started in 1907, but mainly developed in the 1920s. There is as yet no Anning Road nor council estate.

61. A rather later view from the east of Woodmead Road, with the first houses, in a Frith of 1909. The tallest building to extreme right is Higher Mill. Slopes Farm, recently given to the Woodland Trust, stands isolated in its fields.

62. This part of Lyme, known in local slang as Monkey's Rough, now Windsor Terrace, is where the once persecuted Baptists tended to settle away from the main town. Some of their older names, Jordan, Jericho, Paradise Fields, are more poetic. The square building in the distance is Higher Mill, now flats.

63. A closer view of the second old cottage in the last photograph. The old man was said to be a Hallett, who named his sons Shadrach, Meshach and Abednego. The cottages have all gone.

64. North, Manor and South Avenues in 1929, from Slopes Farm. Colway Lane goes up the hill in the trees above. The slang name for this area in its early years was 'Chinatown'. The building of council houses all along this north-east side of the Lim has greatly changed Lyme in this century.

65. (Left) The old Sherborne Lane with its cobbles, now gone. The cottages on the left were demolished in the 1950s, but the taller house, Eagle House, survives.

66. (Below) The cottages, Sherborne Lane. Though all once thatched, they are less old than most people think. They were hastily built in the 1790s, to meet Lyme's sudden rise as a tourist resort. The double-gabled building at the end was once a pub, the Crown and Anchor.

67. (Opposite top) Upper Broad Street, by Godlee, about 1901. The old Sherborne Lane may just be seen to the left. This area was once known as the Top of Town.

68. (Opposite bottom) A little lower. The central building, Monmouth House, was Roberts' well-known boys' school, and is now the Post Office. Its garden once ran down almost to the Lim.

Broad Street

69. A Frith of 1909. The two buildings to the right were once part of the Great House, the most important building in Broad Street. The central Elizabethan porch was demolished in 1913. The part to the left is now Boots. The passage just beyond, leading to Pitt House, now a baker's, was modernised in 1924. The once familiar gatepost eagles have disappeared.

70. Adam's the greengrocers, the little house formerly on the site of Woolworths. The narrow passage to the right led to Govier's celebrated forge behind. Carts could only be taken into it by lifting them on their side.

1. *(Above)* Lower Broad Street, about 1920. The lost Shambles market was against the wall leading to the Island (or Middle Row) entrally. The old Assembly Rooms, demolished in 1928, may be glimpsed beyond it.

2. *(Following page)* The south-west side of Upper Broad Street. It shows many well-known houses. The one by the second cart is Junster's, Lyme's main publisher through the 19th century. Below that the brick building was the imposing residence of the Raymonds, vho largely "managed" Lyme for the Fanes up to 1830. Just below that may be seen an oval shop sign. This little house was where Mary Anning lived from 1826 to her death in 1847.

73. A modern photograph by Paul Penrose of the Island and the seaward end of Broad Street. The lights of West Bay twinkle to the eas

74. The Royal Lion in the 1890s with its coach serving the station – which would have been at Axminster in those days.

75. The Royal Lion briefly 'tudorised', a Frith of 1906. The original 16th century Lion was an inn back in what is now its yard, to the left.

76. Artillery volunteers passing through Lyme on their way to camp, perhaps in the 1870s, a photograph by J. Walter. The telegraph pole of the old Post Office may be seen on the left.

77. The same scene, largely without people. The house extreme left still survives, but all those up to the Three Cups Hotel were destroyed in the 1889 fire. The leftmost of those was the one advertised here.

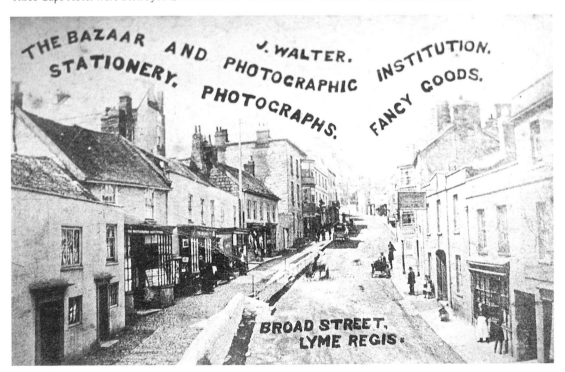

78. Rendall's Grocery beside Temple House to the right. Above is Farnham's, which used to make ammonite jewellery. Drake's Way now passes between the two shops. Rendall, the father of Rosa, was several times Mayor. The Museum holds his photograph collection.

79. *(Below)* The western half of the Assembly Rooms, perhaps in the 1880s, formerly on the site of the Cobb Gate car park. The bow-fronted window at the end of the Island above has long been a sweet shop. The donkey may come from the Cement Works at Monmouth Beach, where they were once much used.

80. *(Below)* The demolition of the Assembly Rooms in 1928, as seen from Bell Cliff steps. This was of the Victoria Hall, the western half. The Assembly Rooms had originally been warehouses. Photograph by Miss Parham.

81. Opened in 1901, the Alexandra is now the doyen of Lyme's hotel industry.

82. The back of the Alexandra. A Frith of 1906. In the past it had been a Dower House for Earl Poulett and belonged to William Pinney, father of Lyme's first Reform M.P. Much earlier still its site may have been the manor house of the ancient Sherborne Abbey estate on the west bank of the Lim.

83. Demolished houses in Silver Street.

84. Upper Silver Street (from Latin *sylva*, a road leading to the woods). The little square opening in the wall is a dipping place from the times when an artificial gutter (shute lake) ran down the street. William Morris stayed in the first house right, with the railings, in 1883. The window next door was Blanche Palmer's. The house with the thatched porch and pavement railings at the end was Morley Cottage, the home of the famous Miss Philpots, three sisters who began collecting fossils here from 1805. It is now the Mariner's Arms Hotel.

85. The Victoria Hotel, opened next to the station, photographed in 1907. The railway opened in 1903, closed in 1965. Before and after that railway passengers had and have to use Axminster, opened from 1860.

86. *(Left)* A Frith of 1930. The Vicarage, Sidmouth Road, was built in the early 1850s for Hodges' occupation. From 1888 to 1899 it held St Michael's College for clergymens' sons. Coram Tower, on the corner just below, was built in the 1890s to house the masters. This building is now called Coram Court.

87. *(Below)* The Woodroffe School. The building, by the Hallett brothers, began in 1929. It was opened in 1932, about the time of this photograph.

88. A photograph of the old Cottage Hospital, a little way above the last photograph on the Sidmouth Road, at Keble Cottage. It moved here in 1886, then to The Gables in 1897.

89. An entry for Lyme Carnival, perhaps against an oil-slip, shows the present Ken Gollop's father. There is an old tradition of sarcastic humour in Lyme, perhaps best exemplified in its formidable collection of less than perfectly polite nicknames.

Sea Lyme

Can one think of town and element apart? Lyme has always lived and still very largely, though in changing ways, lives off the sea. The Cobb is first recorded in writing in 1294, but is certainly earlier. Salt-making goes back to the Dark Ages, the sea-trading zenith came between 1500 and 1700, its seaside resort self first began to flourish about 1760 ... today's visitors, strolling round the Cobb with all its modern pleasure craft, might remember how very different things once were. They are treading a kind of ancient Cape Canaveral, which once launched countless voyages into the unknown. In the 1670s Lyme had greater Customs receipts – and presumably trade – than Liverpool.

90. *(Above)* This aerial photograph of the Cobb shows something many casual visitors do not realise: how close it is to one of the last great wild stretches – the Undercliff – on the south coast. The county boundary with Devon follows the first long hedge running inland from the cliff.

91. *(Following page)* A familiar view of the Cement Works, Monmouth Beach, with its brick kiln and the Cobb and its hamlet from the late 1890s. Both the brick kiln and the Cement Works were soon to end. The long roof behind the conical kiln was the first lifeboat house of 1869; the new house of 1884 may be seen nearer the Cobb directly behind.

92. A ship drying its sails at the landing quay, perhaps in the late 1890s. The little girl sitting by the derrick is the Little Rose of Lyme, Rosie Rendall.

93. Mrs Emily Boswell standing on Granny's Steps, a famous feature of the Cobb. Some think, almost certainly wrongly, that these are the steps Jane Austen made Louisa Musgrave fall down in *Persuasion*.

94. Paddle steamer trips along the coast, from Weymouth as far as Exmouth, were popular in earlier Lyme. Here, about 1905, one approaches the Victoria quay, added to the old Cobb in the 1840s. The pile of stones marked with a post was typical of those collected by the stoneboatmen, for later picking up as ballast.

95. *(Above left)* Local fishing continues at Lyme. Roger Mayne's photograph of a local French-built trawler, the *Whynot*, with the Cobb slope behind.

97. *(Above)* Another photograph of 1973 by Roger Mayne of the modern Cobb. It shows the Portland stone, right, with which it was clad during the early 19th century rebuilding. The piles in the harbour to the left are not mooring posts, as many suppose, but once carried the old truckway round to the landing quay.

96. *(Left)* The Cobb in 1924. The densely tree-clad slope behind preceded the serious slipping in 1962 at the hands of a foolish developer. The dark house on the beach belonged to Wyatt Wingrave until he died in 1938. The long building behind the flag-pole was originally a store. The new Cobb Arms pub now stands in its place.

98. *(Above)* An early Frith, probably of 1892. The closest cottages belonged to the coastguards, the house extreme left to their chief officer. Ozone Terrace, begun in 1890, is not yet complete. The 1869 lifeboat house may be seen right, with an open door. In the Cobb itself, the little cluster of boats at the end of the North Wall are stoneboats. They always moored here.

99. *(Left)* The Cobb square in the early years of of this century. The modern lifeboat house now stands here. The men in uniform are coastguards. Lyme was their headquarters on this coast in former times. Smuggling was rife well into the 19th century. They left Lyme in the 1920s.

100. *(Right)* The coastguard watch-house, at the foot of Cobb Road. It was formerly on the Cobb itself. Just above may be seen an inn sign, that of the old Cobb Arms. The slate-clad house is still existent.

101. From half-way down the Cobb Road, perhaps in the 1880s. The road was once a private road, mainly serving workers at the shipyard at the bottom, active until 1850. The tennis courts to the left satisfied the rage, considerable in Lyme, for the new sport in later Victorian times.

102. A Frith of 1890. Houses just to the right of the previous photograph. The instability of this road, first opened in 1832, has long been a Lyme nightmare. The first house in this row has had to be demolished. The third cottage down, on a corner, belonged to Captain Sir Richard Spencer, a half-pay naval officer who in 1833 went to West Australia as governor of the little colony at Albany, near Perth. He and his large family lived in this small cottage, in typically (for old Lyme) cramped conditions.

103. The running out of the lifeboat from the 1884 house in Cobb Square, which is not yet built up. A Cement Works' chimney may be seen in the background, finally blown up in 1936. The lifeboat was the *Susan Ashley* until 1915 and thereafter the *Thomas Masterman Hardy*.

104. The *Susan Ashley* being launched. Positions in the volunteer boat were coveted. One such man was dismissed the crew for drunkenness. His family dreaded lifeboat maroons, as the poor man always got drunk again for shame.

105. The Cobb from the north-east in the 1890s from the former grounds of Cliff House. The quantity of sailing ships in the Cobb was by no means unusual throughout the 19th century.

106. The Bay Hotel was built in 1924, Sundial House next to it in 1901. Next to that is Library Cottage of the 1830s; and next to that Argyle House, an early sea-baths of the same date. The jetty before the hotel is known as Lucy's, but was originally conceived and promoted by the geologist De La Beche.

107. A late Victorian photograph of the east end of Cobb Bay leading up to the Assembly Rooms at the end. The Lower Walk was also known as the Cart Road and was to help the Cobb porters get their 'plows' (carts) across the shingle to the Cobb.

108. An early photograph, probably of the 1880s, of bathing machines on Cobb Bay beach. The steps leading down to where they stand are still known as Bathing Machine Steps.

109. Bathing Machine Steps may be glimpsed just beyond the lamp post in this Edwardian photograph of 1912. The Toms family seem to have first introduced the idea of tents to Lyme about 1905. The Municipal Council were painfully shocked that some dissolute people were actually undressing openly on the sands.

110. Promenading on the Walk (as older residents still call the Marine Parade) at the turn of the century. This exercise was once so popular, at least among middle class residents, that it was almost like an Italian *passegiata*.

111, 112. The best known row on the Walk is the thatched one surrounding Madeira Cottage of about the 1820s. This photograph may look innocent, but the lower picture shows that the end cottage, Little Madeira, was added to match the rest in 1935-6.

113. A photograph of 1922 from the Cobb Gate Jetty. It shows the two parts of the Assembly Rooms, demolished in 1928. The one on the right was latterly a cinema. The ancient Cobb Gate, through which all goods had once to pass to be assessed by the Customs, lay between them and the dark building in the centre. Note the striking effect jetties have on beach levels. The tidal drift here is from west to east. The town walls were mainly put up in the 18th century.

114. The Cobb Gate in the 1890s. Beyond may be seen the long jetty-piles before Gun Cliff and the Drill Hall (Marine Theatre). The Guildhall, marked by a fleche, is hidden by other old buildings, long demolished. The gap between them and the building extreme left (once Bennett's Baths) was of the demolished house where Mary Anning was born. The Museum is now here.

115. A 1946 photograph by Margaret Woods of a heavy sea at Cobb Gate.

116. Back Beach, on the east side of Gun Cliff. The lump at the bottom of its wall, still just visible in 1990, is the last relic of Guise's Wall, which once enclosed land round the present Marine Theatre. Back Beach was by tradition the preserve of the Curtis family.

117. The Red Arrows over the Cobb in post-war days. Their annual visits are much welcomed by the grockles, if not always so kindly by the residents. Another photograph by Roger Mayne.

In Foreign Parts

118. Once anywhere outside the old Municipal Borough boundaries was counted foreign. The old Black Dog, Uplyme, is the first pub in Devon. It had its name from a lane behind, and echoes one of the oldest themes in English folklore, that of Black Shuck, a demonic dog. The Hound of the Baskervilles legend is related to it, though the Uplyme Black Dog had a kinder image.

119. *(Above)* A meet of hounds, probably the Cotley or the Axe Vale harriers, outside another famous local inn, on 28th February, 1899.

120. *(Right)* Another view of 1911 of where the meet was. It is a simpler form of the Hunter's Lodge Inn just north of Lyme.

121. *(Below)* A Catholic sailor was cruising in Lyme Bay when he saw an old house inland, and swore he would buy it. In 1830 he did so. His name was Sir John Talbot (who died in 1861); the house, Rhode Hill in Uplyme. This is an early photo of the original Georgian mansion that Admiral Talbot bought.

122. Chimney Rock in the 1890s. It is a famous landmark, now largely hidden under ivy and other foliage, overlooking Lyme from the west. Stonebarrow and triangular Golden Cap may be seen along the coast.

13
Co
the

13
– i
Pa

123. Underhill Farm, also just in Devon, and its dairy have been a favoured walking place from Lyme since Jane Austen's day. It is now in severe danger because of landslipping.

H.M.S. Formidable

136. The battleship *Formidable*, of 15,000 tons, was torpedoed early on New Year's Day, 1915. Of the 780 crew on board, nearly 550 officers and men drowned. It was the first major U-boat loss of the First World War. In bad weather only three lifeboats got off. One, with some exhausted survivors and some dead, finally landed at Lyme. They were taken to the Pilot Boat Inn.

137. The *Formidable* lifeboat landed near where the boy is standing. There was some rather unpleasant bickering after the event concerning the role a Sergeant Stockley of the local police played, or did not play, in the rescue. He was given a medal, in some eyes not deserved.

138. The most famous story connected with this tragedy concerns a mongrel dog called Lassie, belonging to the landlord of the Pilot Boat. Those believed dead were laid in a separate room there. In the chaos Lassie crept up and began licking the face of the corpse of a Seaman Cowan. He suddenly stirred. He was not dead. This faded newspaper photograph of 1915 shows Cowan and his saviour.

139. Lassie. Though only cross-bred, she became so famous that her name transmigrated to Hollywood and became attached to a canine film star.

"LASSIE"
THE FAMOUS DOG WHO SAVED THE LIFE OF COWAN
FROM H.M.S. FORMIDABLE.

The Railway

140. Photographs of the railway are numerous and have been published elsewhere, so we will not repeat them here. Proposals for a line to Lyme went back into the 19th century. This shows the station in the early years of this century.

141, 142. *(Below and opposite page)* The opening day, 24th August, 1903.

143. The Cannington Viaduct in Uplyme, the most famous part of the run from Axminster. Its building was commenced in 1901. It still makes a significant landmark in the countryside behind Lyme. In one of the fields close behind lies the Roman villa at Holcombe, perhaps the most ancient local manmade relic.

144. Axminster station, showing the old footway across the track. The little Lyme-line engine stands beside the much larger main-line one.

Finale

145. "Porchway to the Sea", a photograph by A. Chatwin. This view of the beach through the iron trellis of No. 4, The Walk, is from one of Lyme's most attractive Victorian houses. A reminder that Lyme can, though not alas during the usual holiday season, be almost angelically mild and peaceful.